DEDICATION

To all those who strive for fulfillment in their careers,

This book is dedicated to you.

May its pages offer guidance, inspiration, and support

as you navigate the twists and turns of your professional journey.

Your dedication to finding meaning and satisfaction in your work

inspires us all to reach for our highest aspirations.

May you find fulfillment, purpose, and joy

in every step you take towards your dreams.

This is for you.

Bhopal

Retire with Confidence

Your Roadmap to a Secure and Fulfilling Future

Riley Anderson

Copyright © 2024 RIley Anderson

All rights reserved.

CONTENTS

ACKNOWLEDGMENTS 1
CHAPTER 1 1
Envisioning Your Dream Retirement 1
    1.1 Defining Your Ideal Lifestyle 1
    1.2 Location, Location, Location 2
    1.3 Financial Freedom vs. Frugal Comfort 3
CHAPTER 2 5
Assessing Your Current Financial Landscape 5
    2.1 Income Streams 5
    2.2 Expenses and Debts 6
    2.3 Financial Assets 7
CHAPTER 3 9
The Power of Early Planning 9
    3.1 Time is Money 9
    3.2 Setting SMART Goals 10
    3.3 Building a Retirement Budget 11
CHAPTER 4 13
Employer-Sponsored Retirement Plans 13
    4.1 Understanding Your Options 13
    4.2 Contribution Strategies 14
    4.3 Vesting Schedules 15
CHAPTER 5 17
Building Your Investment Arsenal 17
    5.1 Risk Tolerance Assessment 17
    5.2 Diversification is Key 18
    5.3 Mutual Funds, ETFs, and Individual Stocks 19
CHAPTER 6 21
Social Security: A Safety Net, Not a Lifeline 21
    6.1 Understanding Eligibility and Benefits 21

6.2 Maximizing Your Social Security Benefits........................... 22
6.3 Social Security and Taxes... 23

CHAPTER 7.. 25
Unveiling the Mysteries of Medicare...................................... 25
7.1 Parts A, B, C, and D... 25
7.2 Supplemental Insurance.. 27
7.3 Planning for Long-Term Care Costs..................................... 28

CHAPTER 8.. 30
Keeping Up with Inflation: Strategies to Secure Your Purchasing Power. 30
8.1 The Eroding Power of Inflation... 30
8.2 Investment Strategies to Combat Inflation....................... 31
8.3 Retirement Income Streams that Adjust for Inflation.............32

CHAPTER 9.. 34
Estate Planning: Protecting Your Legacy................................34
9.1 Wills and Trusts..34
9.2 Power of Attorney and Beneficiary Designations.................... 36
9.3 Minimize Estate Taxes.. 37

CHAPTER 10.. 39
Embracing Your Golden Years: A Guide to Fulfilling Your Retirement Dreams..39
10.1 Staying Active and Healthy... 39
10.2 Engaging in New Pursuits..41
10.3 Finding Purpose and Meaning.. 42

ABOUT THE AUTHOR.. 44

ACKNOWLEDGMENTS

I would like to express my heartfelt gratitude to everyone who contributed to the creation of this book.

First and foremost, I am deeply thankful to my family for their unwavering support, patience, and encouragement throughout this journey. Your belief in me has been a constant source of strength.

I extend my sincere appreciation to my friends and colleagues who provided valuable insights, feedback, and encouragement along the way. Your perspectives enriched this project in ways I could never have imagined.

I am grateful to the mentors and educators who have guided and inspired me with their wisdom and expertise. Your mentorship has been instrumental in shaping my understanding of career fulfillment.

A special thank you to the readers who have embraced this book. Your curiosity and eagerness to learn motivate me to continue sharing knowledge and insights.

Lastly, I want to acknowledge the countless individuals who have shared their stories, experiences, and expertise in the field of career development. Your collective wisdom has laid the foundation for this work, and I am deeply grateful for your contributions.

Thank you all for being part of this journey.

CHAPTER 1

Envisioning Your Dream Retirement

Retirement – the golden years, a well-deserved break from the daily grind. But what does that truly mean for you? This chapter is your starting point, a roadmap to crafting your perfect retirement vision. Here, we'll delve into the key aspects that will define your ideal post-work life.

1.1 Defining Your Ideal Lifestyle

Imagine yourself – free from the constraints of a work schedule. What fills your days with joy and purpose? This is where you paint a vivid picture of your ideal retirement lifestyle. Consider the following:

- **Activities and Passions:** Have you dreamt of learning a new language, mastering photography, or finally tackling that novel you've been putting off? Retirement allows you to pursue your passions with gusto. Think about hobbies, creative endeavors, or volunteer work that sparks your enthusiasm.

- **Social Connection:** Are you a social butterfly or a quiet soul who thrives in solitude? Consider how you want to connect with others in retirement. Do you envision joining clubs, traveling with friends, or spending quality time with family?
- **Health and Wellness:** Retirement is a time to prioritize your well-being. Think about activities that keep you physically and mentally active. Will you join a gym, take up hiking, or simply relish daily walks in nature?

By reflecting on these aspects, you'll gain a clearer understanding of what brings you fulfillment and how you envision spending your time.

1.2 Location, Location, Location

Your dream retirement might not be confined to the four walls of your current home. Location plays a crucial role in shaping your post-work life. Here's what to consider:

- **Urban Oasis or Tranquil Escape:** Do you crave the

cultural buzz of a city or the serenity of a rural setting? Think about your preferred pace of life, access to amenities, and proximity to loved ones.

- **Climate Considerations:** Are you a sun-seeker or do you yearn for cooler climes? Factor in weather patterns and seasonal changes when choosing your retirement haven.
- **Cost of Living:** The cost of living can vary significantly depending on location. Understanding your financial situation will help you determine a place that offers a comfortable lifestyle without exceeding your budget.

Exploring different locations, either virtually or through visits, can provide valuable insights into whether a place aligns with your vision.

1.3 Financial Freedom vs. Frugal Comfort

Retirement is often synonymous with financial freedom. But what does that truly mean for you? Here, we explore two key approaches:

- **Financial Freedom:** This entails having enough

passive income, such as investments or pensions, to cover your desired lifestyle without relying on work.

- **Frugal Comfort:** This approach focuses on living a fulfilling life within your means, potentially through downsizing your living space or prioritizing experiences over material possessions.

There's no right or wrong answer. The key is to be realistic about your financial situation and set achievable goals.

By considering these aspects, you'll be well on your way to crafting a retirement vision that reflects your unique aspirations and financial realities. Remember, your dream retirement is within reach – start planning today!

CHAPTER 2

Assessing Your Current Financial Landscape

Now that you've envisioned your ideal retirement, it's time to take stock of your current financial situation. This chapter will guide you through a comprehensive assessment of your income streams, expenses, debts, and assets – the building blocks of your personalized retirement plan.

2.1 Income Streams

Understanding your current income sources is crucial for planning your retirement. Let's explore the different categories:

- **Employment Income:** This is your primary source of income, including your salary, wages, and any bonuses or commissions.
- **Retirement Savings:** This includes contributions to

employer-sponsored plans like 401(k)s or IRAs, as well as any personal retirement savings accounts.

- **Social Security:** Social Security benefits provide a safety net for many retirees. You can estimate your future benefits by visiting the Social Security Administration website (https://www.ssa.gov/).
- **Pensions:** If you work for a government agency or some corporations, you may be eligible for a pension that provides monthly income after retirement.
- **Investment Income:** Dividends from stocks, interest from bonds, or rental income from properties can contribute to your overall income stream.

By listing all your current income sources, you'll gain a clear picture of the financial foundation you're building towards retirement.

2.2 Expenses and Debts

Just as important as income is understanding your outgoing expenses. Here's a breakdown of key areas to consider:

- **Essential Expenses:** These include housing costs (mortgage or rent), utilities, groceries, transportation, and healthcare.

- **Discretionary Expenses:** This encompasses everything beyond the essentials, such as entertainment, dining out, hobbies, and travel.
- **Debt:** Outstanding debts such as mortgages, student loans, or credit card balances can significantly impact your financial picture. Knowing your interest rates and minimum payments will help you strategize for repayment.

Creating a detailed budget that tracks your income and expenses will reveal areas where you might be able to adjust your spending or find room for saving more. Remember, every little bit counts in preparing for a secure retirement.

2.3 Financial Assets

Your financial assets represent the resources you've accumulated over time. Here's what to include in your assessment:

- **Retirement Accounts:** The value of your 401(k), IRA, or any other retirement savings accounts will play a major role in your financial security post-retirement.

- **Investment Accounts:** Stocks, bonds, mutual funds, or real estate holdings contribute to your overall net worth.
- **Cash Savings:** Emergency funds and readily available cash can provide peace of mind and cover unexpected expenses.
- **Equity in Your Home:** The value of your home, minus any outstanding mortgage, can be a significant asset.

Taking inventory of your financial assets provides a snapshot of your current financial strength and helps you determine how far you are towards achieving your retirement goals.

By meticulously examining your income streams, expenses, debts, and assets, you'll gain a clear understanding of your current financial landscape. This information serves as the foundation for crafting a personalized roadmap to your dream retirement in the following chapters.

CHAPTER 3

The Power of Early Planning

The magic of compound interest is often likened to a snowball rolling downhill – it starts small but gathers momentum over time. The same principle applies to retirement planning. The earlier you start, the more time your money has to grow, putting you on a stronger financial footing for your golden years.

3.1 Time is Money

The concept of "time value of money" is crucial in retirement planning. Here's why starting early is so beneficial:

- **The Power of Compound Interest:** Compound interest allows your money to grow exponentially. When you invest early, your earnings also generate returns, accelerating your wealth accumulation.

- **The Benefit of Time:** Starting young gives you more time to ride out market fluctuations. Even if you can only contribute small amounts initially, consistent saving over a longer period can lead to a substantial retirement nest egg.
- **Flexibility:** Early planning allows you to adjust your strategy as needed. If you encounter unexpected expenses or career changes, you have more time to adapt your savings goals or investment approach.

The sooner you begin planning, the more control you have over your financial future. Don't wait until retirement is just around the corner to take action.

3.2 Setting SMART Goals

Having a clear vision is essential, but translating that vision into actionable steps is what truly propels you forward. Here, we'll explore the concept of SMART goal setting:

- **Specific:** Clearly define your retirement goals. Instead of a vague desire for "financial security," aim for a specific target retirement age or desired annual retirement income.

- **Measurable:** Establish benchmarks to track your progress. This could involve setting milestones for your retirement savings or investment portfolio value.
- **Attainable:** Be realistic about your goals and timeline. Consider your current income, expenses, and risk tolerance when setting achievable targets.
- **Relevant:** Align your retirement goals with your overall life vision. Ensure your financial aspirations support your desired lifestyle and priorities.
- **Time-bound:** Set deadlines for achieving your goals. This creates a sense of urgency and keeps you motivated on track.

By setting SMART goals, you transform your dreams into a concrete roadmap for a secure and fulfilling retirement.

3.3 Building a Retirement Budget

Now that you have a clear understanding of your current financial landscape and SMART goals, it's time to create a realistic budget for your retirement. Here are the key considerations:

- **Estimated Retirement Expenses:** Research the typical cost of living in your desired retirement location. Factor in essential expenses like housing, healthcare, and utilities, as well as discretionary spending on hobbies and travel.
- **Adjusted Lifestyle:** Consider potential changes to your lifestyle in retirement. You might downsize your living space, travel more frugally, or require less healthcare as you age.
- **Inflation:** Don't forget to account for inflation, the rising cost of goods and services over time. Factor in an inflation rate to ensure your retirement savings maintain their purchasing power.

Creating a retirement budget allows you to assess if your current income streams and savings plan will be sufficient to cover your anticipated expenses. This knowledge empowers you to make informed decisions and adjust your strategy if needed.

By embracing the power of early planning, setting SMART goals, and building a comprehensive retirement budget, you'll be well on your way to achieving your dream retirement.

CHAPTER 4

Employer-Sponsored Retirement Plans

Many employers offer retirement savings plans as a valuable benefit to their employees. These plans can be a powerful tool to accumulate wealth for your golden years. This chapter will equip you with the knowledge to navigate employer-sponsored retirement plans effectively.

4.1 Understanding Your Options

There are two main types of employer-sponsored retirement plans:

- **Defined Contribution Plans:** With these plans, you and your employer contribute a specific percentage of your salary to your individual account. The value of your account grows based on your contributions and investment returns. Examples include 401(k)s and 403(b)s.

- **Defined Benefit Plans:** These plans are less common and are offered by some employers, typically government agencies or large corporations. With defined benefit plans, the employer guarantees a specific monthly benefit payment upon retirement, based on a formula that considers factors like your salary and years of service.

Understanding the type of plan your employer offers is crucial for making informed decisions about your contributions and investment choices.

4.2 Contribution Strategies

Maximizing your contributions to your employer-sponsored plan is an excellent way to accelerate your retirement savings. Here are key strategies to consider:

- **Employee Contribution Limits:** The IRS sets annual contribution limits for both employee and employer contributions to retirement plans. Familiarize yourself with these limits to ensure you're contributing the maximum allowed.

- **Employer Matching:** Many employers offer matching contributions, essentially free money that boosts your retirement savings. Contribute at least enough to capture the full employer match. This is essentially like getting a raise on your retirement savings!
- **Catch-Up Contributions:** If you're 50 or older, the IRS allows you to make additional "catch-up" contributions to your retirement plan each year. This can be a great way to accelerate your savings if you started late or haven't been contributing the maximum amount previously.

By understanding contribution limits, taking advantage of employer matches, and potentially utilizing catch-up contributions, you can significantly increase your retirement savings.

4.3 Vesting Schedules

Vesting refers to your ownership rights over employer contributions made to your retirement plan account. Here's how it works:

- **Vesting Period:** This is the time you need to be employed with your company before the employer contributions in your account become fully vested, meaning they truly belong to you.
- **Vesting Percentages:** Vesting typically happens gradually over a set period, often 2-5 years. For example, you might be 20% vested after two years, meaning you own 20% of the employer contributions made to your account so far. If you leave the company before becoming fully vested, you may forfeit some or all of the employer contributions.

Understanding your plan's vesting schedule is crucial. If you're considering changing jobs, it can impact how much of your retirement savings you'll be able to take with you.

By familiarizing yourself with the different types of employer-sponsored plans, contribution strategies, and vesting schedules, you can leverage these powerful tools to build a solid foundation for your retirement dreams.

CHAPTER 5

Building Your Investment Arsenal

Now that you've explored employer-sponsored plans, it's time to delve into the world of investments. This chapter equips you with the knowledge to build a diversified portfolio that aligns with your risk tolerance and retirement goals.

5.1 Risk Tolerance Assessment

Not all investments are created equal. Some offer the potential for high returns but also carry a greater risk of loss, while others provide more stability with lower potential gains. The key is to understand your risk tolerance – your comfort level with potential investment fluctuations.

- **Risk-Averse Investors:** If you prioritize security and are uncomfortable with market volatility, you may lean towards conservative investments like bonds or government securities.

- **Moderate Risk Tolerance:** Investors with a moderate risk tolerance might allocate their portfolio across a mix of asset classes, balancing some riskier stocks with more stable bonds and cash equivalents.
- **Risk-Tolerant Investors:** Those comfortable with potentially higher swings in exchange for the possibility of greater returns might allocate a larger portion of their portfolio to stocks, potentially including growth stocks with higher risk-reward profiles.

Understanding your risk tolerance is the first step towards crafting an investment strategy that aligns with your comfort level and retirement goals.

5.2 Diversification is Key

The golden rule of investing is diversification – don't put all your eggs in one basket. By spreading your investments across different asset classes, you can mitigate risk and smooth out market fluctuations.

- **Asset Allocation:** This refers to the strategy of dividing your investment portfolio among different asset classes, such as stocks, bonds, and real estate. The ideal asset allocation for you will depend on your risk tolerance and retirement timeline.
- **Benefits of Diversification:** When one asset class experiences a downturn, another might perform well, helping to offset losses and protect your overall portfolio value. Diversification also reduces your exposure to the risk of any single investment performing poorly.

By diversifying your investments, you create a more resilient portfolio that can weather market ups and downs, putting you on a steadier path to achieving your retirement goals.

5.3 Mutual Funds, ETFs, and Individual Stocks

Now that you understand risk tolerance and diversification, let's explore some popular investment vehicles:

- **Mutual Funds:** These are professionally managed investment pools that hold a variety of stocks, bonds, or other assets. Mutual funds offer diversification and convenience, but come with management fees.

- **Exchange-Traded Funds (ETFs):** Similar to mutual funds, ETFs track a specific index or investment strategy. They trade throughout the day like stocks, potentially offering lower fees than actively managed mutual funds.
- **Individual Stocks:** Investing in individual stocks allows you to potentially pick companies with high growth potential, but also carries a higher degree of risk, as the performance of your portfolio hinges on the success of those specific companies.

Each investment vehicle has its own advantages and disadvantages. Understanding these options allows you to construct a diversified portfolio that aligns with your risk tolerance and investment goals.

Remember, this is just an introduction to investment options. Consider consulting with a financial advisor for personalized investment advice tailored to your unique circumstances.

CHAPTER 6

Social Security: A Safety Net, Not a Lifeline

Social Security is a vital social safety net program in the United States, providing retirement income to eligible individuals and their dependents. However, it's crucial to understand that Social Security benefits are not designed to fully replace your pre-retirement income. This chapter will equip you with the knowledge to navigate Social Security and maximize its role in your overall retirement plan.

6.1 Understanding Eligibility and Benefits

To be eligible for Social Security retirement benefits, you must have a minimum number of work credits earned through Social Security taxes paid on your income. The specific number of credits required depends on your birth year. You can find detailed information and eligibility requirements on the Social Security Administration website (https://www.ssa.gov/).

The amount of your Social Security benefit is based on your average indexed monthly earnings (AIME) over your 35 highest-earning years. You can estimate your future benefits using the Social Security Administration's online tools.

It's important to remember that Social Security benefits may be subject to taxation depending on your total income.

6.2 Maximizing Your Social Security Benefits

Here are some strategies to maximize your Social Security benefits:

- **Work Longer:** The longer you work, the more years of earnings are factored into your AIME calculation, potentially increasing your benefit amount.
- **Delay Claiming Benefits:** You can start receiving Social Security retirement benefits as early as age 62, but for each month you delay claiming past your full retirement age (FRA), your benefit increases. This can be a good option if you expect to live a

long life or have other sources of retirement income.
- **Maximize Your Earnings:** Higher lifetime earnings translate to a higher AIME and potentially a larger Social Security benefit.

By understanding eligibility requirements, benefit calculations, and these maximization strategies, you can ensure Social Security plays its optimal role in your retirement income plan.

6.3 Social Security and Taxes

A portion of your Social Security benefits may be taxable depending on your total income, including other sources like pensions or investment income. The Social Security Administration website provides a tool to estimate how much of your benefits may be taxed (https://www.ssa.gov/).

Understanding the potential tax implications of Social Security benefits allows you to plan your overall retirement income strategy more effectively.

Social Security is a valuable program that provides a

foundation for many retirees. However, by viewing it as a safety net, not a sole source of income, and by implementing strategies to maximize your benefits, you can ensure it plays a supportive role in your overall retirement plan.

CHAPTER 7

Unveiling the Mysteries of Medicare

Healthcare is a crucial consideration in retirement planning. Medicare, the federal health insurance program for Americans aged 65 and over, plays a significant role. This chapter will equip you with the knowledge to navigate Medicare's different parts and explore options for supplementing your healthcare coverage.

7.1 Parts A, B, C, and D

Medicare is a complex system with various parts that cover different aspects of healthcare. Here's a breakdown of the key components:

- **Part A (Hospital Insurance):** This covers inpatient hospital stays, skilled nursing facility care (short-term), hospice care, and some home healthcare services. There is typically a deductible for each benefit period.

- **Part B (Medical Insurance):** This covers outpatient care like doctor visits, preventive services, some medical supplies, and ambulance services. Part B has a monthly premium and typically requires copayments for covered services.
- **Part C (Medicare Advantage Plans):** These are private insurance plans offered by approved companies that provide coverage similar to Parts A and B, often bundled together. Some Advantage Plans also include additional benefits like dental or vision coverage. These plans typically have monthly premiums and may have network restrictions.
- **Part D (Prescription Drug Coverage):** This is optional coverage for prescription drugs obtained through a Medicare-approved plan. Part D plans have monthly premiums, deductibles, and copayments that vary depending on the specific plan you choose.

Understanding the different parts of Medicare and their coverage details allows you to make informed decisions about which parts best suit your healthcare needs.

7.2 Supplemental Insurance

While Medicare covers a significant portion of healthcare costs, it may not cover everything. Supplemental insurance, also known as Medigap plans, can help bridge the gaps in coverage. Here's what to consider:

- **Medigap Plans:** These standardized plans offered by private insurance companies help pay for deductibles, copayments, and coinsurance charges associated with Original Medicare (Parts A and B).
- **Benefits and Costs:** Medigap plans have varying levels of coverage and come with corresponding premiums. Choosing the right plan depends on your specific needs and budget.
- **Alternatives:** Some Medicare Advantage Plans may offer some of the benefits traditionally covered by Medigap plans. Carefully compare plan options to find the most suitable coverage for your situation.

Exploring supplemental insurance options can provide you with additional peace of mind and help manage out-of-pocket healthcare costs in retirement.

7.3 Planning for Long-Term Care Costs

Long-term care refers to the services needed for individuals who require assistance with daily living activities due to chronic illness or disability. Medicare generally does not cover long-term care costs, which can be substantial. Here are some strategies to consider:

- **Long-Term Care Insurance:** This is a specialized insurance policy designed to help cover the costs of long-term care services, either at home or in a facility. Premiums can vary depending on factors like age, health, and desired coverage.
- **Asset-Based Long-Term Care Planning:** Some individuals may utilize asset-based strategies, such as long-term care riders on life insurance policies or Medicaid planning, to potentially qualify for government assistance with long-term care costs. It's crucial to consult with a financial advisor specializing in elder care planning to explore these options.
- **Family Communication:** Having open conversations with loved ones about your preferences and potential long-term care needs can

ease the burden on them in the future.

Planning for long-term care costs is an essential aspect of securing your financial future in retirement. By exploring various options and having open communication with family, you can develop a strategy to address these potential expenses.

By understanding the different parts of Medicare, supplemental insurance options, and strategies for long-term care, you can navigate the complexities of healthcare coverage in retirement with greater confidence.

CHAPTER 8

Keeping Up with Inflation: Strategies to Secure Your Purchasing Power

Retirement might seem far off, but inflation, the gradual rise in the cost of goods and services over time, is a constant presence. This chapter equips you with the knowledge to navigate inflation's impact on your retirement savings and explores strategies to ensure your purchasing power remains strong throughout your golden years.

8.1 The Eroding Power of Inflation

Imagine a basket of groceries costing $100 today. Due to inflation, that same basket might cost $110 next year and $121 the year after. Over time, inflation erodes the purchasing power of your money. This is a crucial factor to consider in retirement planning, as your fixed income needs to keep pace with rising costs.

The impact of inflation can be significant. For example, if you underestimate inflation by just 1% per year, your retirement savings could lose 26% of their purchasing power over 30 years. Understanding this concept allows you to develop strategies to combat inflation's effects on your financial security.

8.2 Investment Strategies to Combat Inflation

Here are some investment strategies that can help your retirement savings outpace inflation:

- **Growth-Oriented Investments:** These investments, such as stocks or real estate investment trusts (REITs), have the potential for higher returns than inflation, potentially preserving your purchasing power. However, they also carry higher risk.
- **TIPS (Treasury Inflation-Protected Securities):** These government bonds offer a guaranteed principal amount that adjusts for inflation, ensuring your purchasing power is maintained. However, TIPS typically offer lower returns than traditional

stocks.

- **Asset Allocation:** A diversified portfolio that includes a mix of asset classes, including some inflation-resistant options like stocks and TIPS, can help mitigate risk while potentially keeping pace with rising costs.

By incorporating these strategies into your investment plan, you can increase your portfolio's resilience to inflation and ensure your savings maintain their value throughout your retirement.

8.3 Retirement Income Streams that Adjust for Inflation

Certain retirement income streams automatically adjust for inflation, providing peace of mind and helping maintain your purchasing power:

- **Social Security Cost-of-Living Adjustments (COLA):** Social Security benefits are typically adjusted annually based on the Consumer Price Index (CPI) to account for inflation.
- **Some Employer Pensions:** Certain employer

pensions might offer annual adjustments to benefits based on inflation metrics.

- **Annuities with Inflation Riders:** An annuity is an insurance product that provides a guaranteed stream of income in retirement. Some annuities offer optional inflation riders that increase your payout over time to keep pace with rising costs.

Understanding which of your retirement income sources adjust for inflation allows you to plan your overall spending strategy more effectively.

By implementing these strategies, you can mitigate the impact of inflation on your retirement savings and ensure your purchasing power remains strong throughout your golden years. This proactive approach allows you to maintain your desired lifestyle and enjoy a secure and fulfilling retirement.

CHAPTER 9

Estate Planning: Protecting Your Legacy

Retirement planning isn't just about securing your financial future; it's also about safeguarding your legacy. Estate planning ensures your wishes regarding your assets and loved ones are carried out after you're gone. This chapter equips you with the knowledge to create a comprehensive estate plan that protects your legacy.

9.1 Wills and Trusts

A will is a fundamental estate planning document that outlines your wishes for the distribution of your assets after your death. Here's what to consider:

- **Asset Distribution:** Your will specifies who inherits your belongings, such as property, investments, and personal items.

- **Guardian for Minor Children:** If you have minor children, your will can designate a guardian to care for them in the event of your passing.
- **Executor Appointment:** The will also names an executor, the trusted individual responsible for managing your estate and ensuring your wishes are fulfilled.

While a will is essential, it may not be suitable for all situations. Trusts offer additional benefits and flexibility:

- **Trusts:** These legal arrangements allow you to transfer ownership of assets to a trustee who manages them for the benefit of designated beneficiaries. Trusts can avoid probate, a court process for validating wills, which can be time-consuming and public.
- **Types of Trusts:** There are various trust types, each serving a specific purpose. For example, revocable living trusts offer flexibility in managing assets during your lifetime and distributing them upon your passing. Irrevocable trusts can help minimize estate taxes.

Consulting with an estate planning attorney can help you determine the most suitable combination of wills and trusts for your unique circumstances.

9.2 Power of Attorney and Beneficiary Designations

Beyond wills and trusts, other legal documents play a crucial role in estate planning:

- **Power of Attorney:** This document grants another person (your attorney-in-fact) the legal authority to act on your behalf in financial or healthcare matters if you become incapacitated. There are different types of power of attorney, each with varying scopes of authority.
- **Beneficiary Designations:** These designations allow you to specify who receives the benefits from retirement accounts, life insurance policies, and other assets upon your death. This can help ensure a smooth and efficient transfer of assets outside of probate.

By having these documents in place, you can safeguard your assets and ensure your loved ones are cared for even if you're unable to make decisions yourself.

9.3 Minimize Estate Taxes

While not everyone's estate will be subject to estate taxes, it's still wise to consider strategies for minimizing them:

- **Understanding Tax Thresholds:** The federal estate tax only applies to estates exceeding a certain threshold amount, which is subject to change. Familiarize yourself with the current exemption to determine if your estate falls within the taxable range.
- **Tax-Advantaged Accounts:** Assets held in retirement accounts like IRAs and 401(k)s typically have tax advantages upon withdrawal by beneficiaries. Maximizing contributions to these accounts can help reduce your taxable estate.
- **Gifting Strategies:** There are annual gift tax exclusions that allow you to transfer assets to beneficiaries tax-free. Consult with a tax advisor to explore gifting strategies that comply with regulations and minimize your estate's taxable value.

By understanding estate tax implications and exploring minimization strategies, you can ensure a larger portion of your legacy passes on to your loved ones.

Estate planning is not about predicting the future; it's about taking control and ensuring your wishes are respected. By creating a comprehensive plan that includes wills, trusts, power of attorney designations, and potential tax minimization strategies, you can safeguard your assets and provide peace of mind for your loved ones.

CHAPTER 10

Embracing Your Golden Years: A Guide to Fulfilling Your Retirement Dreams

Retirement isn't just about financial security; it's about embracing a new chapter filled with opportunities for personal growth, exploration, and enjoyment. This chapter delves into essential lifestyle adjustments to consider as you transition into your golden years and helps you pave the way for a fulfilling and enriching retirement experience.

10.1 Staying Active and Healthy

Maintaining a healthy lifestyle is crucial throughout your life, but it becomes even more important in retirement. Here's why staying active matters:

- **Physical Health Benefits:** Regular exercise

strengthens your body, improves cardiovascular health, and reduces the risk of chronic diseases. Aim for a combination of strength training, cardio, and flexibility exercises to maintain physical well-being.

- **Mental Acuity:** Physical activity has been shown to enhance cognitive function and memory, potentially reducing the risk of dementia.
- **Overall Well-being:** Staying active boosts mood, reduces stress, and increases energy levels, contributing to a more fulfilling retirement experience.

Explore activities you enjoy, whether it's walking, swimming, dancing, or joining a fitness class. Consider joining a health club or finding an exercise buddy for motivation and social interaction.

Prioritizing healthy eating habits is equally important. Focus on a balanced diet rich in fruits, vegetables, whole grains, and lean protein sources. Regular checkups with your doctor are essential for preventive care and early detection of any health concerns.

By making healthy choices and staying active, you can

enhance your physical and mental well-being, setting the stage for a vibrant and fulfilling retirement.

10.2 Engaging in New Pursuits

Retirement offers the freedom to explore passions and interests that may have been put on hold during your working years. Here are some ideas to spark your creativity:

- **Learning New Skills:** Take a cooking class, learn a new language, explore photography, or delve into creative writing. There are endless possibilities to expand your knowledge and develop new talents.
- **Travel Adventures:** Always dreamed of visiting Italy? Now's the time to embark on that adventure! Research destinations, explore travel options that suit your budget and interests, and create lasting memories.
- **Volunteer Work:** Give back to your community by volunteering your time and skills. This can be incredibly rewarding and provides opportunities to connect with others who share your passions.

- **Hobbies and Interests:** Dust off that guitar, join a book club, or start a vegetable garden. Nurture your hobbies or discover new ones that bring you joy and a sense of fulfillment.

Retirement is an opportunity to reinvent yourself. Embrace new experiences, explore hidden talents, and pursue activities that bring you excitement and purpose.

10.3 Finding Purpose and Meaning

Beyond leisure activities, consider how you can find deeper meaning and purpose in your retirement years. Here are some ways to connect with your values and contribute to something larger than yourself:

- **Mentoring:** Share your knowledge and experience with younger generations by becoming a mentor in your field or volunteering with youth organizations.
- **Community Involvement:** Get involved in local initiatives, participate in civic activities, or advocate for causes you care about. Making a positive impact on your community can be incredibly rewarding.
- **Family Time:** Retirement offers the opportunity to

spend more quality time with loved ones. Strengthen family bonds, travel together, create new traditions, and cherish these precious moments.

- **Personal Growth:** Retirement is an ideal time for introspection and reflection. Explore personal development opportunities, engage in spiritual practices, or pursue self-improvement goals that contribute to your overall well-being.

Finding purpose in retirement doesn't have to be grand gestures. It's about connecting with your values, contributing to something meaningful, and creating a sense of fulfillment that transcends your professional career.

By prioritizing physical and mental health, engaging in new pursuits, and finding purpose, you can transform your retirement from mere leisure into a vibrant and enriching chapter filled with personal growth, meaningful connections, and lasting memories. Congratulations on reaching this exciting new phase of life!

ABOUT THE AUTHOR

Riley Anderson is a multifaceted individual, blending the roles of business guru, writer, and motivational speaker. With a keen insight into the intricacies of publishing and a talent for inspiring others, Riley has become a sought-after figure in both the literary and entrepreneurial worlds.

In terms of education, Riley holds a degree in Business Administration with a focus on Marketing from a reputable university. This educational background, coupled with years of practical experience, has equipped Riley with the knowledge and skills needed to navigate the competitive landscape of both the business and publishing industries. Whether through written works or captivating speeches,

Riley's aim is to empower and guide individuals on their journey to success

www.ingramcontent.com/pod-product-compliance
Lightning Source LLC
Chambersburg PA
CBHW050244230526
45470CB00005B/2102